# HADRIAN'S WALL

## (Vallum Hadriani)

*poems by*

# Albert Flynn DeSilver

*Finishing Line Press*
Georgetown, Kentucky

# HADRIAN'S WALL

## (Vallum Hadriani)

Publisher: Leah Huete de Maines
Editor: Christen Kincaid
Cover Art: Hadrian's Wall by Marian Cremin, © 2015
Author Photo: Albert Flynn DeSilver
Cover Design: Elizabeth Maines McCleavy


Order online: www.finishinglinepress.com
also available on amazon.com

Author inquiries and mail orders:
Finishing Line Press
PO Box 1626
Georgetown, Kentucky 40324
USA

# Table of Contents

# HADRIAN'S WALL
### (Vallum Hadriani)

I set upon the Roman bounds neither of space nor of time. I have
bestowed upon them empire without limit. . .to impose the ways
of peace, to spare the defeated, and to crush those proud men
who will not submit
—Virgil (as spoken via the supreme god Jupiter)


*Animula, vagula, blandula*
*Hospes comesque corporis*
*Quae nunc abibis in loca*
*Pallidula, rigida, nudula,*
*Nec, ut soles, dabis iocos.*

*Little soul, gentle and drifting,*
*guest and companion of my body,*
*now you will dwell below*
*in pallid places, stark and bare;*
*there you will abandon your play of yore.*
 *But one moment still, let us gaze together*
*on these familiar shores, on these objects*
*which doubtless we shall not see again....*
*Let us try, if we can, to enter into death*
*with open eyes...*

—Emperor Hadrian 138 AD (translated by Margurite Yourcenar)


*Poetry transformed me: initiation into death itself will not carry me*
*farther along into another world, than does a dusk of Virgil*

—Emperor Hadrian (via Margurite Yourcenar)

## MILECASTLE I
*—Remus*

Days begin with the ringing
of a great bronze bell
built from our suffering, built
of blackness between
rank reminding, birthing
of sparks, tiny boats
afire in the blood, float
the burnt length of the throat
empty mouths burp up
charcoal holes who
sing forth such space, rape
under stars, broken
teeth, mirrors blooming
like spiked white flowers, our
only hour, where
our crying origins
arise

# MILECASTLE II
### —Hadrian

My earliest memory, like a tomb
seated naked at the bottom
of a freshly dug
grave, making mud
pies with my fated Spanish
hands, nothing but pale
gray smoke and fog
above, a single white
gull scissoring through—
four black dirt
walls, memory's suspended
emptiness beneath me—
somehow I was held
afloat in that pit,
nourished by wet earth,
planted by wind as if
a weak little seed,
polished by the promise
of the sun, to be both lit up
and burned to ash
an oblivious point
of starlight, hoping not
to be buried alive
by the soils
of age
and empire

# MILECASTLE III

How to make a poem
from a history of rubble?
Stones piling up like words
heaped on stone, heaped on word
upon word, heaped on memory
upon memory, heaped on sun, heaped upon moon
fact run through the ringer, fact run aground,
through the agenda-grinder
of the mind, heaped upon fact
heaped upon bias, "my ass," heaped upon
conditioning stuck to the mind like barnacles
stuck to the hull of the Mayflower,
run aground upon Dedham granite
(off the coast of Gloucester, say or Carthage, Solway Firth)
the weight of dead granite ideology—
Maximus of Tyre, Emperor Hadrian, my
measly Milecastle watchman. . .who
at the helm is headed toward Plymouth
Rock, headed toward Hadrian's wall
trying to right this ship of state
running aground on the borderlands
of language. Watch those thoughts (rocks)
jut out (the Farallon Islands, Olson's Babson Ledge,
that jagged shelf off Palmarola in the Tyrrhenian sea)
ideas and knowledge sharpening an edge
building up from ocean bottom birthing
a wall between us, between you and you—
oh how history sticks. History, his story,
what about hers—what about theirs,
between you and you, there is a field. . .
between yoni and lingam, between you and them
you and the universe, being beyond
"the measure of things," here on the outer banks
mulling about in the "undone business" insisting
as it does, clank, clank, birthing itself ad infinitum,
spilling amniotic ink—just to see the sea before me

(the battered self) in woodland sky
looking up between Redwood trees stretching out
from my feet, to eternity and back, that Junco bird,
this instant, just her thought, her word

## MILECASTLE IV
*—Lucius*

Ode to Northumbria in November
in seventy-three songs (miles, or so)—
I am but a storied man,
a soldier to Hadrian's army to
serve and protect the great empire

a volunteer from the Isle of Sicillia, Augusta's
coastal waters, scrub lands of dry
straw, sent to the frontier, the wet north lands
of Barbarian peasant castle kingdoms

no contest for the trained men of Rome, center
of the world. Here we meet the wild Barbarian
rife with Viking blood, minds of ice,  hearts
of frost, light limping from tired eyes
bent by the tilt of frozen earth. . .

Terror, whose error, hate in their hearts, a wall
we shall build to keep such beasts
at bay, behind civilized lines, from here we shall
call forth the superior man, the superior race
celebrate the conqueror's creed, be strong,
be strong in Roman song and deed!

## MILECASTLE V
*—Remus*

Cliffs of the Whin
Sill, be my barrier
be the land before me
how it ripples geologically
like the wavelets of an
indrawn tide (a great god
breathing) be the cleft
corrugations of one land
laughing, North of Hexham gap
where two continents
collided some ungodly
time ago (a wink in an
emperor's eye)
thrusting rock crusts
upwards, burping cobbles
for my masons to stack . . .

\*

The smoke from a thousand
fires plumed into Northumberland skies
to fire the kilns, endless
men needed to burn stone
supply the blacksmiths
and quarrymen, their
sandpits, laborers laborers,
laborers, slaves, slaves and more
slaves—pitch your tent
behind a palisade
or wherever you can
muster, keep the men
in check, well fed and drunk
pack in the heavy
rock on ox carts, gather
the skilled mason-men
around the arches
work the flax ropes and pulleys

place the block
and tackle hoists, lift
the arch stones and hope
the rope don't shear
under the weight of
Whin or lime stone
crux, if so chisel
me down with the rough
claws or quick nippers
to grip it; bullnoses, gougers,
nickers and punches to set rock,
quick, quick, we've got a wall
to build

## MILECASTLE VI
*—Hadrian*

Hadrian, oh Hadrian
I say it's got to be a song, a canto,
a chorus of serrated
voices, a cup, a coup, a canticle
a ring upon a conquered land—

I think of the Greeks and get weepy
about the great chariot races,
Mt. Olympus, that wussy Jupiter we stole
as our god to claim, how our own games
came. . .gladly we built the Gladiator arena
at the coliseum, a field full of blood on Sundays
to cull the herd as it were
slay the slaves I say, but beef
up the arts and infrastructure.
I inherited the idea, don't blame me
it was the Democrats, I mean the Republicans,
no the Republicrats with their stiff senate
rules, crazy hats. Hey who makes the rules
around here anyway? Oh, I do, all the undoing—
a fool who concentrates all the wealth
and power and water and meat in my small meaty
hands—notwithstanding, shall burn off
all ten fingers, all ten toes
Oh how all I touch turns to
ash and dust
and so I will build monuments and walls
for you to remember me by,
because I can't stand not to exist
I can't stand it even after death,
in all it's living terror, the wall—
when it's gone all gone, and I'm gone
and what remains are my remains,
and the rain remains
eternity arising, with each wet
drop of life the tyranny and totality
of presence persists!

## MILECASTLE VII
*—Lucius*


Of rock-clump built by time, lookout looking out
keeping time to tough duck flight-flap and wind whistle,
lemony clips of sunlit wings how they catch

the underside of feathers tracing the high divides,
the no-escape escarpments, cut off swales,
fields of vast purple heather, vales, sheep-swept
and clamoring over hill and dale, like stray white
thoughts. . .memories of the old country's tawny
sea cliffs, ocean song, I've gone pasty-white with longing. . .

I watch gangs of men in angled armor
now clanging up slick slopes, disappearing, no hope
but in breathing through rain-beaten days, grasses,
glassy eyed, wet with sweat, look out, look out
see only bird and cloud clutter gather now

not another soul or animal for miles if ever, look
south to a fork of the river Tyne, names named by
Roman throats, twisting through lofty troughs,
keeping time to gale-light, fierce falcon wing,
the dreamiest of things

beat back boredom's arrow, molasses hours, drenching
rain relentless wind, keep out, keep out repetitive steps
atop the stone turret, remember to keep those brute Barbarians,
Norse invaders, tax evaders at bay

keep in tact the Empire's iron hand, a minute crack
in a ship's hull can sink a great ship, shit, who's coming?
A band of stags in the brush, a rush of quail flushing upwards,
a break in the clouds, loud shafts of sunlight breaching boredom's
slate

look out, look out, between old castled estates, light fading, fires out,
a wall of night nestles in. . .just shards of silver starlight now define

## MILECASTLE VIII
*—Lucius*

I write to you from my Milecastle, my
castle-castle, my wall, my hall, my cell,

my tomb of pure arising. What looms in my feet
as I pace the cold stones, what catapults through

a loose mind at rest [an elegy to freedom
from the point of enclosure]

as the night knots up the dark, thief of my seeing
what has become of the angels within me?

they have scattered in the thin void of quick dark
I am left to my non-devices pressed to this emptiness

this weed-lot of thought, thicket of thorns
memories tangling up the land in unclaimed brambles,

a nighthawk shrieking in its sleep, multiple
animal nightmares or simply the truth of midnight being

a cry of longing, a lengthening. . .from my listening
grows an altar to this moment, in praise of the temporary

me a mere wave lapping up against time
this infinite instant—grave temple of the night

## MILECASTLE IX
*—Lucius*


Here at the frontier
my warrior's life
chalked up to flickers
of sleep on the heaths,
moon-less night
watch under thick
damp, a rare fist
of crisp stars
burning blue rings
around the hurried
clouds. . .


I count my days off with thin provisions
lists inked on sap wood; a rabbit or two, tough boar,
mead, gathered roots and berries, herbs
wild lettuces, spicy greens, barley stacks

keep track of shouting commands, rock clack, earth dug
slave drives. Make sure the jousts are sharp
spears pointed out. Off wall, see a rogue
Barbarian approach the wall, blast the bugle call

trigger a regiment of horses sent, inspire a
charge of men, then to see was just
a stray peasant chasing deer along
the north face of the wall. . .

Trying not to list the fraught tangle of my clawing
at my mind, missing my family my flotilla of lost loves
fastened to distant shores

## MILECASTLE X
*—Lucius*

My first week up in the Milecastle, when
the first snows arrived and the frosts insisted,
we went inward hunched within our patchwork
of fox fur, leather, and thin skins. Built small
fires in the corner of our tower. That's when
the Barbarians rushed us, in snow and ice,
they're made of it, that and elongated dark.
We men of the Mediterranean made of
sun and warm volcanic stone, fresh from Vesuvius.
They had us caught cold off guard, drowsy
with frosted brows, bleary after days of wet sleet.

The wall was breached by a rogue band
of fifty, took over the fifty first turret,
stabbed ten Roman men, pillaged our provisions,
tossed them off the south side of the wall
in a leathery heap. Word was slow, but when it came,
the legions rushed forth with a vengeance
seldom seen, surrounded them easily
from the outer flanks, reclaimed the turret.
No need to starve or burn them out,
the cavalry with a back force of legionnaires closed in
at close range stabbed and bludgeoned them
one by one with superior spears and clubs,
forced the last bunch to beat their own
mates to a pulp right before us. Just as
fifty black starlings burst forth
from the frozen elms, as if asking the emperor
to hear the thin screaming
from their wings

## MILECASTLE XI
### —Remus

Dear Beloved emperor,

Half of me is ocean, half of me is sky
Half of me is sparrow-hawk on winged
time, half of me is wind.
Half of me is lava flow, half of me is stone
half of me is river eddy, half of me is dream. . .

At times the wall disappears
underneath my feet into polished
pebbles, shiny grains of song.

Oh the meaty bleats of silence
behind thought, where space
is clenched in time's smoky fist

Let the hidden angels twist
and shift, and lift upon the layered lands
and let the keen echoes ring with
an infinite Roman wind.

To be immersed in thickets of being
therein, ecstatic flares of awareness
sparking fires on the spine
each vertebrae prickling in the heat of thought

Sightlines speak through charcoal
explosions of starlings
startled off the Linden tree, drift in peppered
waves of flake, and flee—

Vague blue veins in my eyelids squirm
small worms, words. . .poked out by

Pin-pricks of dream; blood-want, wine
sex and death, the hidden eyes of the Barbarian
night—oh how the grinding wheels of the wall roll on

## MILECASTLE XII

Now I too
am an alien
immigrant other, a
*fiend in a cloud*
a loud leaning
drifting over the
wall, the emperor, the
empire, like a tuft
of ash from a soldier's
funeral pyre, a dire wolf
feeding at a fleeting,
feeling, flying forever
higher and higher

# MILECASTLE XIII

To be embodied as the walled
one, as stone, as wall or
stone slayer, to be
embodied as river, to be
as wind, as mind, to be a player
embodied as night, as slight breath
to be embodied as sting or shout
across the heath to be
embodied as stretch and flow
of moonlight, to be embodied, as raft and lift
of air, as hawk wing might, to be
embodied as falcon shriek and drift
as tower or sliver of quick frost to leaf
to be embodied as bone-cold hour
as sun spire, thread of lava-hope to be
embodied as fox or bear fur, as open boat
taken with wave, to be embodied as
wince or frown to be embodied as jewel upon
a crown to be embodied as crow or raven mind
of the deathless divine
to be embodied in odes as monk face flower
or waning hour to be embodied
as the mountains weep or even sleep, to be
embodied as starlight's creep to be
embodied at the cold throat of time
coughing up a dragonfly's line, to be
embodied on the tongue of a thrush, hunkered
down in the brush, to be
embodied at autumn's rest at the breast
of death's chilly gate, to be
embodied in the song of hate

beyond the urge to kill at the plate
to be embodied walking death's dark dare
breath by breath, in wait, to be
embodied repeatedly there to be
embodied here, in the lookout tower
of doubt, hour by hour looking
overly inward at the cutting
edge of I, to be embodied to the vastness
of the sky inside, that distant star,
to be embodied just
as you are

## MILECASTLE XIV
### —*Atticus*

I was a soldier once and now I am an egg
at night, reborn on the other side of beginning

as a bygone Barbarian zygote Cyclops
single eye, that other guy
wooly uncivilized animal that I am

seeing myself as one man merging therein
the shadows of the sun
one soldier, lost my sword there in the fight
lost my breastplate and iron clad helmet
lost my stone bearings there,
lost my seeing, went naked in the thickening dark

One wall advancing on me as a warrior does
one morning, spears of sunlight piercing
one Milecastle lookout, a glass vise tightening
around the egg, my heart, the longing & loss
that connects us, one long night
of looking outward
staring into the singular dark
one moon-lit spaceship of mind
colliding with the stars
and what appears to me, a Barbarian Roman egg,
him and me disappearing
into daylight into a single scrambled thing

## MILECASTLE XV
*—Lucius*

I dreamt of her
and her hours
almost daily she,
a whisper, dusk's vesper
a wisp or avatar, the girl
from afar I saw
at the foot of the wall,
all of her in vision
if only her blonde curls
curling inward toward me
her golden brow, green eyes
asquint in the low autumn
sun. Pitched atop a high
cliff seaside we, the running
white cliffs at Dover, swath
of swifts over and over
in darting traces scattered
behind her bright hair,
as if originating there in
untethered nests
I see you. . .your
scarf of silk filament,
winsome sea-foam skin. . .
said eyes looking out, looking
as a watchman watches
the wall always outwardly
blinded by our very seeing,
how the watching washes
what's seen away. . .muffled thunder
of doilied waves below, frail
air salted to tongue
wet with longing for the length
of her, no walls between us
as she radiates within me
sunlight spires, the horizon
line has collapsed behind her
like a sexual sigh. . .have I
even begun to love you, the years,
and your disappearing.

## MILECASTLE XVI
*—Lucius*

Some young Barbarian
prat showed up in the colluding
dark between Milecastles,
nightly escaping our sights,
sat scratching into Roman rock,
his mark, a petroglyph picture,
of a Barbarian boy holding
a string tied to a cloud
his feet dangling at an odd
angle in no air as if being
lifted by a brute
wind, up and over
the wall

# MILECASTLE XVII
*—Cynwrig*

We Celts, Scots, Viking war-bandies
animal cults, we Caledonians, people
of the raven smearing ourselves in our
mothers, sisters, daughters moon-blood
before battle protecting our dirt for seventeen
hundred summers, our men have fought
for our women, children, heaven, for dirt, for razed stone
for our fellow people of the raven, beyond care
for air, earth, death, or water where we're hell-bent
on oblivion, blasting into battle, fearless against
empire, the charge of Roman might, we keep them
back to the Northumbrian hills, let you build a wall there
to keep your Barbarian southern sun-worshipers
from our sacred north. We draw the line and let you
build it, go ahead enslave the Brits and Picts to break backs for it
there is no capturing our people of the air our
raven people fight from beneath the quick dark
wavering between realities, memory, membranes
We of the other dimensions can travel to & fro upon
blank wings cleft to no thing, our bodies are our arrows
not ours, impossible to kill, we are not a soldier but an instant
of illusion, the mere mirage of a man, a filament, figment
of your weary Roman imagination. We are mere thought
of human meat, appearing as adversary, opposition, as a
fleeting blink before your sun-drunk Mediterranean eyes
you are blinded by this physicality, you stab and pierce
pound and plunder, driving yourselves further under
you have no spear or sword, no catapult that can pummel cut
and kill the night, with your flimsy arsenals you cannot murder
the air, your might, and swipe and shot is mute against
our shape and shift, no chase can catch us on swift obsidian wings

## MILECASTLE LIV

Looking to spot
the rare vermillion flycatcher
I went birding at Organ Pipe
Cactus National Monument
just south of the town
of Why. The force of air
across the border, raging—song
of the organ pipe, song of little
water, the flycatcher thrives
on a couple drops of nectar, keeps
its chipper trilling up, its song
of open crossing, open
airways, void of walls, thought
I heard its distant song but no sighting
though through a borrowed border guard's
unguarded scope I spotted
a young girl barefoot in a vermillion
poncho stumbling through an arroyo,
I swear I heard her weary
song something about
having to crawl out from under
the body of her long-dead
mother, the only shade for miles,
she sang

## MILECASTLE LVI
*—Lucius*

Who am I to deny
this wall of tears? This gift
of stacked rock of nature's
split song, Hadrian's
vast will to defend, reeking
of god's grace to bend, to
displace, and destroy
as well as build and bloom.
As with fingers full of sunlight
stabbing down new babyshoots
sprouting from scorched earth,
a song sung across the bow
of a dead soldier's brow
creation, oh sweet creation. . .
*all one wave of notes in the dark*
slave song, emperor's song
song of moonlight foaming
at the mouth of night,
can't you hear us crying?

## MILECASTLE LVII

Is anything
barrier? Thought or wall
for instance it's rock
or wire, razor face,
height, the guards their
guns or bludgeon
sticks supposedly made
of mostly space. Atom. Space.
Atom. Space. Atom.
Space. Adam, the border guard
at Tijuana who misses
his mother. Atoms Blinking
off and on so fast as if
to be mere theory. "Later, mom." Specificity
can't help them,
the type of rock; igneous,
schist, lime, granite or quartz or
their uniforms of leather,
tin rivets, iron helmets,
cheap Chinese nylon. Color
just collapses in a sanguine
heap there at the foot—
the way the sun glints off
of things, sounds of metallic
clamor, allow entry only
cloud—white, scratch
your name in the stone
face, face the dissolve, wind
and rain will eat your
identity there, and then what
other, other is left there,
to keep out?

## MILECASTLE LVIII
*—Lucius*

All that is holy
flows over the wall
as words or cloud,
that sparrow—

loneliness of the middle
hour silently, the losses
piling up with age, a returning
sun, pays no mind.

What is it to gather
our sorrows
like flecks of time
broken sticks of moonlight?
to love what is splintered
as much as the sublime

only your song
that mysterious push of feathers
can tether us to the holy,
can fully remind.

## MILECASTLE LIX

Polyhymnia, oh great goddess
of sacred poetry and mime
sing to me in real time,
send me some sacred hymns
of the divine, a song from the
beyond, beyond time—
a song rushing forth from
the swimming-pool-Malibu-blue
sky, from the screeching beaks
of those wild parrots
parroting through, from the tip
of the brown onyx Aracanthus leaves
birthing the carved marble
boy next door, or that exquisite
cinerarium chest leaving us
breathless as if therein lay
our very own ashes—I ask
you whose ashes last 2,000
years, this instant, I ask ashes
what rises up from such dust
flowing from the folds
of your cold marble toga,
from your folded arms tucked
within, right hand under chin
hidden folds of filament skin—
what makes the asking of ashes
possible? What is the hymn
of the invisible thin? That which
makes this beaming marble body
possible, or even mine, my
pyre-bound body, as I bow down
now in asking, going up
in flames of inspiration
before you!

$A$lbert Flynn DeSilver is a poet and prose writer, speaker, and workshop leader. He received a BFA from the University of Colorado and an MFA from the San Francisco Art Institute. Albert served as Marin County California's very first Poet Laureate from 2008-2010. He is the author of several books of poems including *Letters to Early Street*, and his work has appeared in more than 100 literary journals worldwide. Albert is also the author of the memoir *Beamish Boy*, which was named a "Best Book of 2012" by Kirkus Reviews. His latest nonfiction book, *Writing as a Path to Awakening: A Year to Becoming an Excellent Writer and Living an Awakened Life*—based on his popular writing workshops by the same name—was published by Sounds True in 2017. Albert is also a teacher and speaker having presented with U.S poet laureate Kay Ryan, bestselling authors Cheryl Strayed, Elizabeth Gilbert, Maxine Hong Kingston and many others. He teaches writing at literary conferences nationally. More information about his work can be found at www.albertflynndesilver.com.

www.ingramcontent.com/pod-product-compliance
Lightning Source LLC
Chambersburg PA
CBHW022101080426
42734CB00009B/1453